Sam And The Mysteries Of Shadows

The Discovery

Shreyan Binu

Chennai • Bangalore

CLEVER FOX PUBLISHING
Chennai, India

Published by CLEVER FOX PUBLISHING 2023
Copyright © Shreyan Binu 2023

All Rights Reserved.
ISBN: 978-93-56485-93-8

This book has been published with all reasonable efforts taken to make the material error-free after the consent of the author. No part of this book shall be used, reproduced in any manner whatsoever without written permission from the author, except in the case of brief quotations embodied in critical articles and reviews.

The Author of this book is solely responsible and liable for its content including but not limited to the views, representations, descriptions, statements, information, opinions and references ["Content"]. The Content of this book shall not constitute or be construed or deemed to reflect the opinion or expression of the Publisher or Editor. Neither the Publisher nor Editor endorse or approve the Content of this book or guarantee the reliability, accuracy or completeness of the Content published herein and do not make any representations or warranties of any kind, express or implied, including but not limited to the implied warranties of merchantability, fitness for a particular purpose. The Publisher and Editor shall not be liable whatsoever for any errors, omissions, whether such errors or omissions result from negligence, accident, or any other cause or claims for loss or damages of any kind, including without limitation, indirect or consequential loss or damage arising out of use, inability to use, or about the reliability, accuracy or sufficiency of the information contained in this book.

*This is for you, mom
The Best Mother in the World*

CONTENTS

1. Shadows And Dreams 1
2. Hi Leo 4
3. After I Almost Believed It Was A Dream! 7
4. Fire In The Hole, Literally 10
5. She Hurts To Look At! 13
6. Of Course, The World I Live In Goes Crazy 16
7. Leo Lives In A Mansion 20
8. Rock, Paper, Scissors 24
9. Of Course Glint Has Magic 29
10. Ride With Dogs 32
11. Din 41
12. Am I Dead? 46
13. The King And Queen 55
14. My 'Parents' 60
15. I Finally Use My Magic Somehow 64
16. The Puzzle Room 68
17. Leo's Cars 72

Epilogue *74*

Chapter 1

SHADOWS AND DREAMS

Tick, tock, tick, tock… I counted the times the clock ticked. It was in the middle of the night. Mom and Dad were sleeping and I was not. Something didn't feel right. I got up and went to the bathroom, washed my face and looked in the mirror. I saw my shadow out of the door into the room. I simply stared at it. At that moment, I could swear it was staring back at me. I blinked and it looked like a normal shadow again. I walked out and closed the door. I threw open the window curtain and the street light streamed in and fell on a wall.

SAM'S SHADOW TALKING TO HIM

It was very quiet as I lay on the bed. It was so quiet that my ears started to ring. I looked at my shadow on the wall. It felt like we were staring at each other. I dared not to blink and I held the gaze for a while. But then, I blinked. My shadow looking at me—nonsense! But I still felt a bit weirded out.

I turned to the side, and at that moment my heart stopped. I saw my shadow again, except it was standing and I was not! I would have checked out the window in case someone was there making that shadow, which would not have been any less scary, but the shadow had blue flames for eyes.

I officially stopped working when it spoke, "Hello Sam,"

"Who are you?" I wanted to say confidently but it came out as a squeak, "You who?"

He held up a hand, "Your questions can wait. I know this might come as a shock to you."

This might come as a shock to you, I thought mockingly. Ya think?

"Now before you say anything, I will do what I am here to do and go. So, let me do it. If we shadows weren't there, nothing would exist. We are not copies of you; you are copies of us and always have been."

I don't know what happened but I slowly fell asleep.

Chapter 2

HI LEO

"Sam, wake up! Sam, you are going to be late for school," my mom called.

Despite the lack of sleep, I got up and I had questions. Was the shadow real or not? How did it know my name? What was he trying to say? Why didn't I switch the lights off even though I went back to do it? I pushed all that stuff aside; I had more important things to do. I brushed my teeth and got dressed for the first day in my new school, Redwood School. Yep, even with all drama last night, I had to worry about the first day of school.

Wait, hold it. Before I tell you more of this crazy story of mine, my name is Sam…Sam for Samar. Yeah, my dad's Indian. I'm a total of thirteen years old which is pretty much fourteen, which is pretty much fifteen… too much?

Anyways, I moved to India after completing my seventh grade in the US. We used to stay in the US. but then last year we decided to move to India so that "we could connect to our roots." At least that's what my parents had said.

But now, I was back in the US.

And that's all. So back to the story:

Things will go as they will, I guess. I ate my breakfast and packed my bag. Just as I did, the horn of my school bus blared. "Bye, Mom, I am leaving," I called.

"Bye Sam. Have a nice day at school," Mom replied. I opened the door and got in the bus. I looked for a seat in the back, as was my preference. As I was doing so, I noticed that the bus was packed. There were only a few seats left in the whole bus.

People started to realize that I was a new student and they whispered amongst themselves. Even though I could not hear them, I knew they were talking about me. Soon, they stared at me for some reason as I was choosing my seat. They stared like it was the most important choice of my entire life. Then, it hit me. I knew what was going on, in my previous school my friends had warned me about this. You see every school has ranks and first impressions always matter. So, if I sit with the loners I will become a loner, if I sit with the cool kids, I will become one of them and it is the same with the sporty kids, bullies, and nerds. So, I tried to sit with the decent-looking kids. I finally found two kids who looked normal and so, I sat with them.

I was pretty sure that all three were nervous to talk to each other. The kid next to me took out a red book on which I read 'journal' on the cover. The kid opened the book and started writing in it, "First day at Redwood School. Hope it goes well. Anyways, two kids are sitting next to me and I will sit with them at lunch and try to talk to them. If they are nice, I will become their friend. Ok then, talk to them at lunch."

"So, you are also new?" I asked.

"How do you know that?" the kid asked in shock. "You muttered it," I said.

"Oh, sorry about that. I do that sometimes. My bad. Anyways my name is Leo. What is yours?" Leo said.

"My name is Sam," I replied.

"Nice to meet you, even though I was supposed to meet you at lunch," Leo said enthusiastically. "Huh?"

"Never mind about that."

Way too friendly.

Chapter 3

AFTER I ALMOST BELIEVED IT WAS A DREAM!

Leo and I got off the bus. We looked at the school building.

"Looks like a prison if I have seen one," Leo commented.

I shrugged my shoulders. "Let's go inside and find our lockers," I replied. We both went inside. Once we found our lockers, which were right next to each other, we went to homeroom. We walked in and got seats in the class. The bell rang and the teacher walked in and took his seat behind the desk.

"My name is Mr. Davy and I will be your teacher for the rest of the year," he said the last part like a villain with fingers of his hand together and all. "I wish to keep you sad and tortured—I mean happy and laughing." The bell rang and he said, "So let us start."

I sighed, another bad day, typical for my life. "Is the entire year going to be like this?" I asked Leo.

"It is going to be rough", Leo said as he patted me on the back. The class went by and we got going to our next class as soon as the bell rang.

Leo looked at the timetable and said, "Oh come on! Our next class is 101, the chemistry class." While you might be like chemistry is fun, I found the class boring. You get to play with chemicals and all! A normal chemistry class might be, but apparently, our teacher thought that we were still too small to use real chemicals. So, she prepared water with paint in it for us to use instead. How did I know? I mixed a bunch of "chemicals" and they turned to a really ugly color. The way paint turns if you mix them up. And as you see I found it boring and so, I fell asleep.

This became the mistake of the month because I had a nightmare. A shadow appeared, in my dream of course.

"Remember me?" the shadow asked.

"You are that shadow dude that came in my dream," I said.

The shadow looked irritated, "My name is Sateran, the lead soldier."

"Look dude, I don't know why you are here but I don't want to hear another senseless speech," I said.

"I did not even get to finish the last time. Which is why I am here right now. Ahem" he cleared his throat, "Where was I?" he asked.

"Something about copies."

"Ahh yes, we are not copies of you, you are copies of us. So, the earth is rightfully ours and we will remove those silly pesky humans off the planet. By the way, what do think we should name the Statue of Liberty after we change it into a shadow? Statue of Shade? No, too shady. How about 'The Great Statue of Shadows? Or 'Statue o-"

"Get to the point."

"Alright, alright. So, will you help us destroy the world?"

Chapter 4

FIRE IN THE HOLE, LITERALLY

I was shocked and Sateran said that like it was totally normal. Any normal person will be terrified if you ask them, "Hey, we are shadows and we are on our way to destroy the world. Want to join?"

"I'm waiting," Sateran said impatiently.

"But I am also human so won't you destroy me too?" I pointed out.

"You haven't found out yet?" he asked.

"Found out what?"

"That you are not human. Well, not completely anyways." And for the second time, I was shocked.

"You are half human and half shadow," he said. "Now, will you help us or not?" he asked.

Should I help a villain who wants to destroy the world and possibly me? Hmm... a tough decision.

"No," I said flatly.

"Well then, are you sure? We could rule the world and teach you to use your powers."

"Still a no."

He shrugged his shoulders, "I guess we will have to kill you too. Sam, you have just made a very powerful enemy."

"Sam, Sam, Sam. wake up." I opened my eyes and found Leo slapping me while I was on the floor. "Hey! Don't slap me," I said.

"Oh! I'm sorry. Was I not supposed to wake you up when the whole school is on fire!" he screamed. I got up and panicked looking at everything which was on fire. Fortunately, this included my books, which calmed me down a bit. Just a little bit.

"Come on we have to get out of here!" Leo and I ran for the exit. In the hallways, things were bad, and by bad, I mean very bad. Somehow, the water sprinklers hadn't turned on. I mean, what would you expect, this building might as well be 1000 years old and they just repainted it. Children were crowded in the hallways trampling each other to get to the exit; teachers were trying to herd the children with no luck. Leo and I pushed our way out of the school. There were ambulances, firefighters and cops all around the building trying to extinguish the fire. Even the firefighter club in our school got a fire pipe attached to a fire hydrant but I'm pretty sure they were having a water fight.

Leo and I managed, somehow, to get outside. Thankfully, it was not very big and the fire was extinguished soon. Not many people were hurt. My mom drove in with our car.

She got out and hurried to Leo and me, "Sam! My dear Sam! Are you all right? I heard what happened in the news. Did you get burned or anything? Do you need your teddy bear, Mr. Charles?"

"What?! Ha ha. I don't have a teddy bear. Totally not," I said nervously. Leo turned around to find his own parents. I asked, "Is he in the car?" my mom nodded.

"Who is your friend here?" Leo turned around. "My name is Leo," he said.

"Oh wonderful! Sam is already making friends on his first day of school!" Mom said. "You should drop by our house, Leo. I'll show you all of Sam's baby photos."

I pushed my mom to the car. "Bye Leo. I'll see you tomorrow," I called out. Before Mom could embarrass me more, I made her get in the car with me and drove away.

Chapter 5

SHE HURTS TO LOOK AT!

On the car ride home, I kept thinking about what the shadow had said, "You will die with the other human beings."

When was I going to die? Can I stop it? Probably not. I am just a regular person and they are a whole entire army! Well, Sateran did say something about me having powers, even though I did not know how to use them. There has to be another way. Maybe if I can tell the other people that the shadows are coming… no. They'll think I'm crazy. I don't even know if my dream was real or not. Maybe, it was just a nightmare. Yes, it was just a nightmare.

"What is wrong? Honey?" my mom asked. I realized that I was deep in thought.

"Oh, nothing, Mom," I lied.

"Sam, I know when you are worried. You didn't even tell me off for calling you 'honey.'" She looked at me and said, "You know you can talk to me."

"Mom, honestly, it's nothing."

"If you say so," she said hesitantly. After reaching home, I took a bath and was ready to sleep. Honestly, the day was pretty tiring. So, I did not complain about sleeping a bit early. Try having a dream of a shadow that says, "Hi! You are going to have to die. Have a nice day!" while you wake up and find out that the school you are in is burning. I got tucked in bed and fell asleep after reading a few pages of a book

GLINT WAKES UP SAM

"Wake up, wake up, you lazy bug," a female voice said.

What's with this jolty wake-up call every time? Gimme a break, please!

"Huh," I said groggily. I saw a girl about my age wearing a ridiculous outfit! She wore a blue skirt, orange shoes with black and white striped socks and a pink dress and on top of it, a green jacket with the zip open. She had a mix of red and black hair. And oh boy, trust me, it was not a good combination of colors and to make it worse it was all covered in glitter! I would be okay if it was only one color. And did I say it was a horrible combination? If she went to school, the teacher would have to turn off the light because of her clothes. And as if it was not enough, she had a few small tubes of glitter attached to a string like a necklace, slung around her neck! And remember, I saw it all as my eyes were stinging. I don't think that it is healthy for my eyes to see that as the first thing.

"Come on. We have to leave," She said in a rough voice. She was someone I would not mess with.

Chapter 6

OF COURSE, THE WORLD I LIVE IN GOES CRAZY

*S*o, there I was, looking at a girl with a bad fashion sense. But being the nice person I am, I did not comment on it.

"What's up with the clothes?" Okay, so, I did say a little something. You would have also done that, okay!

"Come on we have to go," she walked towards the door.

"But wait, just because a girl with bad fashion sense barged through my front door in the middle of the night and then tells me to run off with her without telling me the reason or her name does not mean I should do what she says!" "Call me Glint."

"But still! Why? And what kind of parents let their child go out in the middle of the night?"

At the word 'parents,' she flinched. She looked down and I could see water in her eyes. I knew that I had triggered an emotional spot. I swear, I could see the glow of her clothes turn dimmer. "I-I am sorry," I apologized.

She shook her head and looked up. "No, I pity you," she said in a sad voice.

"Why, what happened?" I asked.

"Well, don't get sad. We will save them."

"Save who?"

"Your-" but before she could complete her sentence, my brain connected the dots.

I ran to my parent's room, leaving Glint alone. Please let me be wrong, please let me be wrong. I put my hand on the doorknob. I took a deep breath and opened the door. My heart skipped a beat. "No, no, no!" I said to no one. I ran up to the bed and threw the blankets off. NO! My parents were not there.

"We will save them. So, the sooner we leave, the sooner we will save them," Glint said suddenly.

"But first," I said, "explain everything."

"Alright then, Sam. The shadow you saw in your dreams, Sateran, wanted you for your powers."

Powers again! But I don't have any powers. Anyways, I let her continue, "Because you were not born with powers, you were given powers. What Sateran said was true. There is a world with shadows. Only shadows are given powers, even though, not as strong as you. You are the first human to be given those powers in a million years. And since you were given those powers, they can be taken from you. Sateran plans on taking it from you. And I have heard he has another Safion in his hands. I don't know what he will do, but legend has it that what he will do is going to doom the earth by creating a powerful being, a being so powerful it will bend time itself. Though I don't know what he will do with your parents, I know that I will help you save them," she finished.

"I can't even make a guess of what you are saying but since you know how my parents have disappeared I guess I have no option but to believe you and save them," I replied and headed towards the door.

Glint sighed, "I will explain everything but first, do you even know where to go?"

"Oh." I felt my cheeks getting red. "Where do we go?"

She sighed again, "The shadows can't get out of the shadow realm, but they are growing stronger and will be out soon. I am pretty sure your parents are in the shadow realm. But to get to the entrance of the shadow realm, we have to find the stone."

"Stone? What stone?"

"The stone. It is literally called the stone. Its name was lost eons ago. It leads to the shadow realm entrance. But it isn't that easy to get the stone."

"Where is the stone?"

"It is at the point on earth where the shadow falls the longest just before sunset."

"And where would that be?" I asked

"It's up north from here about a hundred kilometers from here, a place called Romdentia."

Phew! I thought we had to go abroad to somewhere like Australia. I am sure that my allowance for the month would not allow that. "So, anything else I need to know?" I asked.

"No, I think that pretty much sums up everything," she spoke.

"Do we have to take food and stuff?" I asked. "No."

"Let's go then." On the porch, she turned left towards the garage.

"Where are you going?"

"We need transport, don't we?"

"But do you even know how to drive a car? You look twelve years old?"

"I'm sure I will figure it out."

Great, my life is in the hands of a girl who can't pick out her clothes properly. Just great.

Chapter 7

LEO LIVES IN A MANSION

"I think I have to barf," I said as my face turned green. It had been 15 minutes of Glint driving and it had been the most horrifying 15 minutes of my life. It was not only that! She also hit a few lamp poles and fire hydrants. I was starting to think she wasn't even from Earth! I mean, at least you should know what most of the stuff in a car does. Scratch that, at least you should know what a steering wheel does in a car. She literally thought it was a backup shield with holes in it. Anyways, she sighed again. She seems to sigh a lot lately. Or maybe I am the kind of person who makes you sigh.

"Right now?" she said.

"Yes, right now," I said.

"Make it quick." She stopped near one of those modern three stories houses with clean white paint, lots of plants and good lighting.

I hurried out of the car to nearby bushes and looked around to see if anybody was there—there wasn't. I brought my head to the bushes and did my business.

Just as I finished, someone called out, "You know that's my bush, right?"

I swear I jumped five feet high. I looked around and saw Leo looking at me and the bush with his eyebrows raised.

"Oh, Leo. You gave me quite the scare," I said. Hopefully, he did not see what happened before he decided to speak up.

"Ohhh! I am sure it is scary," he said in a sarcastic tone, "scarier than waking up to the sounds of a bush moving in your yard at freaking five o'clock. I finally thought I had caught a monster."

Five o'clock? I looked at the horizon and indeed saw the sun rising. Wait what? The sun is moving towards me? Oh, it is just Glint. Once she was close enough to make out that it was her, the sun came up, the real sun. As soon as the sun's rays hit her, her entire body seemed to shine and not just the part which was hit with sunlight. Well, that is strange. Note to self: in short distances, getting behind the part which was not getting hit by the light is not an option.

"Who is that?" Leo asked.

I was just standing there, dazed by the light. It wasn't that I did not hear Leo's question, I just did not want to take my eyes off the light coming from Glint.

"Hello, hello, hello, earth to Sam," Leo waved his hand in front of me. I blinked a few times and rubbed my eyes.

"Yes?" I asked.

"I was asking who is she and why the heck is she wearing those clothes," Leo asked fishing out a pair of sunglasses. He put them on and stopped squinting. What? Which 8th grader carries a pair of sunglasses in the crack of dawn?

Finally, when Glint reached Leo, in unison they said, "Who are you?"

But Glint said something more, "Who are you, peasant?"

"Excuse me?" Leo said looking offended.

"Excuse me?" Glint said. "You should say that you are sorry for not kneeling before me."

Well, this escalated quickly. "Who do you think you are, a queen?" Leo was boiling with anger.

"Of course, I'm a queen? What do you think you are, peasant?"

I saw Leo going to take a swing at her but sadly, Glint saw that, too, "Oh! Try and hit me but I should tell you that I'm way more experienced in combat than you."

I stepped in between them and held out my hands on the side, "Guys, stop fighting we are on the same side here."

"What?" Leo said, "On the same side for what?"

"I will explain everything but please just stop," I tried to convince Leo. Unfortunately, that just made it worse.

"Sam, you are siding with her? I thought I was your friend."

"Well, umm…"

Was Leo really my friend, I mean, I had only known him for a day. Do friendships form in a day? But being the nice person I am, I said, "Sure, you are my friend. But-"

"Really? You are friends with a peasant, I am disappointed in you," Glint frowned. How can I stop this fight?

"Stop, both of you," I raised my voice. As if by a miracle, they listened.

"By the way, where are you going?" Leo asked. I was about to answer when I realized that I did not know. So, I gestured towards Glint.

"The Den of Din. You probably don't understand. It is the home to one of the most dangerous and oldest creatures. It has the power of a thousand men and goes by a sense of hearing and smell. It stays at a place called Romdentia 100 km north from here. The stone is protected by the creature." Glint finished.

"I always wanted to go camping up north," Leo said.

Leo stopped. A look of excitement crossed his face, "Can I come with you!? My parents are away for the week. It's just me and the butlers in the house. We'll come back before my parents. Please?"

Chapter 8

ROCK, PAPER, SCISSORS

The look on Glint's face was something I couldn't describe. Imagine that your friends have come over to hang out, and they ask to play with your new PS5, you agree but your mom does not. Since, she does not want to be impolite, she gives you a look which clearly says, "Make up an excuse to not play on the PS."

Glint's face was something like that. "No! absolutely not! He is not coming with us." Glint crossed her arms and turned away. Except the fact that she was okay with being rude. Leo looked at me expectantly. I thought for a few seconds. I wanted to say no but he looked so excited. Telling him no would be like breaking his heart. But then there was Glint, too.

"We will decide that through a game," I decided. "If Leo wins, he can come if he wants to. And if Glint wins, she can have it her way. Is that okay?"

"Okay," Leo said. Glint still did not turn. I gave her my deluxe puppy eyes. It always worked on my mom when I wanted her to do something for me, like ordering pizza.

"Alright," she gave in. Inside, I did a happy dance. "What game should I beat this senseless person in?" she asked.

"Rock, paper, scissors."

"What is this rock, paper, scissors?"

"It's-" I began.

But Leo interrupted me, "You wouldn't understand. The game is for normal people, not royals like you."

"It's a simple game," I said ignoring Leo. "You can either take out a rock, paper, or scissors. Rock is like this," I showed her a closed fist, "and paper," I showed her an open palm, "for scissors," I showed her two of my fingers sticking out. "You can take out either of these. Rock beats scissors, scissors beat paper and paper beats rock. Look, I'll show you." I turned to Leo. "Rock, paper, scissors." Leo held out a rock and I held out a paper. "Look, I beat him," I spoke.

"Aha! It's a game of strategy and reading your opponent's mind, a game worthy of me." Thank the gods she understood. I thought I had to explain to her for another hour. Both Glint and Leo held out scissors.

"Now what?" Glint asked. "You redo," I said. "Rock, paper, scissors." This time Glint pulled out a scissor and Leo showed rock.

"Leo won," I said simply.

25

Glint blinked, a look of realization crossed her face, "What this makes no sense! How does a piece of paper beat a rock? Not in a million worlds will this make sense!"

The way Glint erupted, not a single volcano could outmatch her. Scientists could never have seen it coming. Actually, some people might have seen it coming. She blew air and crossed her arms.

"Meet me in the car," she said before turning and stomping away.

"What's her deal?" Leo asked me.

"I don't know. Maybe you both just got off on the wrong foot," I said.

"Maybe. Let's go." We walked to the car.

"Wait," I stopped him.

"What's wrong?"

"We should get some supplies."

"Yeah," Leo agreed. We turned back and walked to the house's front door.

"Now, what?" I asked.

"We have to sneak in, the butlers will ask too many questions and get suspicious. Let's go through the back door. There will be fewer people."

Leo and I made our way to the backyard which was massive. Well, not massive but definitely big. There was lush green grass. A few beautiful trees growing in the middle. Well-trimmed bushes were at the edges before the wall. Whoever made the layout of the garden definitely had good taste. And they also knew where to place the hedges. Get it? Hedges, edges. Bad joke? Got it.

Moving on, Leo and I snuck to the back door. We were careful to duck near the windows so that anyone looking out would not be able to see us. Leo slowly opened the door. And with our luck, the door creaked.

"What's that?" asked a male voice.

"I don't know. Must be the wind. Close the window, will you?" said another

"Duck!" I whispered. We ducked just next to the door, back pressed against the wall. The man peeked outside the door a little bit before closing it.

We got back up again and heard the two men saying, "Let's head for breakfast. It must have started."

"Yeah." They walked away. Leo once again opened the door; it did creak but no one heard it. We slowly snuck in and went straight to the kitchen.

"Get everything you think we need," said Leo. I was really happy. There was so much tasty food! From gummy bears to pizza. It was like a dream. I grabbed some pizzas, snacks and drinks. While I was packing food, Leo was taking some other stuff from a cabinet. It definitely was not food. I decided to not ask. I suddenly heard footsteps coming.

"Let's go!" I whispered. Leo nodded. We quickly headed to the door. As I was leaving, I got a glimpse of the mess we made and also the person coming. In the kitchen, all the drawers and cabinets were left open and food and packets were lying on the floor. It was a total mess! The person coming into the room was a janitor. Yup, a janitor, and he is not going to like what he sees.

"Oh, man!" Leo and I heard as we left. We snickered.

Chapter 9

OF COURSE GLINT HAS MAGIC

Glint was sleeping in the car when we got there. "Let's prank her," Leo said, out of the blue.

"Wouldn't she get mad?" I asked.

"I am sure she will understand."

"But you and Glint are already on a bumpy start, I don't think we should do it."

"Come on! You can hide behind the tree." He gave me his version of puppy eyes, and I got to say, it was better than mine.

"Alright," I gave in. "what prank are we doing?" "I'll throw water on her face," he grinned. Ahh, the good old water on the face. To be honest, I too wanted to see the reaction on her face. I hid behind the tree as Leo got a bucket of water. Where did he get that from? Leo looked at me and gave me a thumbs-up. Slowly, he tilted the bucket. He spilled all the water on Glint and scrambled to hide behind me. That's fine. But what he did next was not fine, he handed me the bucket and pushed me out! Before my slow brain could process what was happening, I was straight in the sight of Glint which was burning holes in me. She was completely drenched with her fists closed tight.

Remember when I said not a single volcano could explode stronger than Glint? Well, after she realized what happened, looking at her made me realize that her full potential was really high. Like a lot. Her last explosion was like a dot compared to this one. Actually, that might be a bit more. But you get the idea. She was staring right at me, not saying a single word. I looked at Leo, giving him a look, which clearly said, "How could you do this to me?" I wouldn't be too surprised if smoke started coming out of Glint's nose. A smile broke out on her face. Sorry, what did I just say? Oh yeah, a smile. Wait what!? A smile! Unless I am mistaken, you smile when you are happy. But surely she can't be happy. I mean, I wouldn't be happy if someone threw a bucket of water on my face.

"Oh, thank you!" she said.

"Why?" Leo came out from behind the tree. "Because he brought my Mageia back," she chimed.

"Your what?" I asked.

"My Mageia. Oh, sorry I forgot that you don't know that stuff, magic. You brought my magic back." I was surprised. But come on! After all this craziness, how surprised can you be? But what I was more shocked about was that she said 'sorry.' She definitely is not the type of person who will say sorry. It might be strange but at least she forgot about the grudge between her and Leo.

"Look at this!" she kneeled before a flower and closed her eyes. Took a deep breath and scrunched up her face. The flower started to grow and bloom. At its full height, it stopped. Glint smiled and got up. The flower seemed familiar. Then, I remembered.

When I was a young kid, my mom handed me a very similar flower. The thing that hurt was that they were not there anymore. The feeling churned inside me. The flower that Glint grew suddenly wilted and died.

"Why did you do that?" Leo asked. Glint flashed me a worried look. I understood then that the powers that Sateran warned me about were activating.

Chapter 10

RIDE WITH DOGS

"You know what?" Glint said.

"What?" Leo asked.

"We should go, we are losing daylight here," she said and walked off to the car.

"Well, that was weird," Leo said. Now, I was going to deal with Leo.

"Why did you push me!" I faced Leo.

"Oh, that doesn't matter anymore. Let's go to the car." He started speed walking to the car. I hesitantly let him go. At least Glint isn't angry at me. I jogged to the car.

SAM, LEO AND GLINT DRIVE TOWARDS ROMDENTIA

"About time, dumbo." And she's back. we started to drive off. After fifteen minutes or so, we had about five near-death experiences, all thanks to Glints driving. Every time that happened, she'd curse in a different language, while Leo and I cursed in English. We had been lucky the last five times, but the sixth time… well, we weren't so lucky.

We were taking a turn on the highway and a truck came from the other way. Any person licensed to drive would have avoided it, but sadly nobody is crazy enough to give Glint a license and I don't blame them. So naturally, we crash. At the impact, the glass shattered and we were sent flying through the windshield.

We landed and rolled beside the highway in a green meadow. I groaned. I'd be lucky if no bones had been broken. My ribs felt like they had been run over by a car. I looked and saw Leo walking towards me. "You okay?" He asked. I stared at him.

"How come you are okay?" I asked.

"Oh, I opened the door and rolled out. I thought something like this was going to happen." I'm so dumb. How come I'd never thought about that?

Somewhere behind me, Glint said, "Now, how are we going to get there?"

"You are asking me? You are the one who crashed the car!" Leo replied angrily. Oh my god! Here they go again.

"Well, your dumb cars in this dumb world are really hard to drive," Glint yelled.

"Well-"

"Stop it!" I ordered. They both fell silent. "You both are arguing like little kids and we are stuck a hundred miles away from home!"

"He's right. Fighting isn't going to help anyone," Glint sighed.

"We need to reach the Romdentia Mountain top ," Leo added. I looked around, and all there was, was a road which stretched into the horizon. I saw a truck stopped by the road. It read, 'Handling of dangerous stray dogs.' And pretty much all grass the other way.

Then I had an idea…

"This is so stupid," Glint commented.

"Yeah," Leo agreed.

"Well, get used to it. It's our only way to Romdentia." Let me explain why we are currently hiding behind large cardboard boxes in a truck which smelled like poop. Well, it began with my idea, which was to hide in a truck which was going towards the Romdentia. But I did not think it was going to smell so bad. Just a tiny setback.

"Hey, Mark. High five, the boss is going to be pleased with us," said a voice from outside. "Aye, Bobby. We've caught a dangerous animal right here," A second voice said. "Hide," Glint whispered. She shimmered and disappeared. Easy for her to say. Leo and I had to cover ourselves in boxes. The doors of the truck opened and light streamed in. It was near sunset. They threw a small cage inside and closed the door. Glint shimmered and became visible.

"How come that's dangerous?" Leo asked. After my eyes adjusted to the dark, I saw what it was. It looked like a dog. Just that made me angry. But when I got a little closer, I got even angrier. It was a puppy—a German Shepherd to be exact. He (I am guessing it was a he) was not in a good state, with his fur all dirty. He looked weak. I decided to get a bit closer. He whimpered and limped to the other side of the cage. I understood his worries; he must not have been treated nicely before.

I knelt down in front of the cage and let out a soothing voice, "It's all right. We aren't going to hurt you." I held out my hand. He still did not trust me.

"Move aside," Leo said. He sat down and held out his hand. Before the dog could react, Leo moved his hand under his chin and scratched it. Slowly, he became comfortable and fell asleep.

"And that's how you do it," Leo said.

"That was cool!" I said.

"Indeed," Glint said.

"How did you do that?"

"Oh, I kind of have a way with dogs. Did I mention I have seventeen rescued dogs at home?"

My mouth fell open. "Ummmm, no." "Anyways, what do we do with him?"

"Her," interrupted Leo.

"I guess it's free to go now," I said. As if understanding me, she whimpered and squeezed Leo's leg.

"Can we keep her?!" Leo asked.

"You won't listen anyways," Glint sighed. "Nope," he said proudly.

Leo snored in the corner with Liz (that's the name of the dog) in his lap.

"So, tell me more," I told.

Glint sighed, "More about what?"

"About these different worlds and me being a Safion and all."

"Okay, let me start at the beginning. It was shadows before humans, all creatures were shadows."

"You mean no one had physical form?" I asked.

"How is that even possible?"

"It was good, until the two clans of shadows, Trophers and Zedexians, had a dispute over control of magic and started fighting. It was not much at first but it escalated quickly." I was as lost as you are but I let her continue.

"It was a raging battle. Many lives were lost. But neither wanted to submit to losing. The situation was desperate and hopeless. One night, in the center of the battlefield, a voice emerged behind a bright golden light. It said that we shadows were no longer worthy of inhabiting Earth. And to prevent us from staying, it became brighter and brighter till it became what we call the sun which turned into the moon at night. The shadows started to fade, gained color and turned into the organisms on the earth today. They even lost all their memories and magic. But the ones who were smart escaped into another realm, now called the 'Shadow Realm.' Even in the Shadow Realm, they divided borders. Now, they each want to reach Earth first so that they can rule it again. Slowly, shadows have found ways to be in the light for a short period of time."

"Like when Sateran spoke to me?" I asked.

"Yes."

"But that still does not explain my magic and why Sateran wants me."

Glint thought about what to say for a bit. I didn't have any problem reading her face because she was literally the only source of light. All I figured out was that she was annoyed I didn't know this already. Yeah, I know. How could I have not known all about shadows which I only first saw a few days ago? Sam, you got a skill issue.

"You are a Safion," she said. "Powers have been given to you so they can be taken."

"So I have been told," I spoke.

"Safions are very rare, their magic is… is different. Since they are rare, little is known about Safion magic. Magic of shadows who have fallen in a certain way, how do you say it, shadows who have fallen but have their purpose unsatisfied get their magic to remain behind and the magic chooses its new owner."

"So, you mean like ghosts," I suggested.

"What are ghosts?" she asked, confused.

"Never mind."

"As I was saying, it is very rare that it chooses a human. So, the magic clashes with human essence and modifies it. There are three worlds in total—Universe, Zedex and Tropher. Universe is here, it is the gateway to both worlds that's why it is called uni-verse and Zedex, it is the home to Scadins. They have magic related to nature and non-violence. Tropher is the home to shadows. They have magic to fight and destroy. Safions have the power of both but which one is more, depends on the person and his intentions. And that's pretty much all."

Strangely I had no questions. "Actually, one question, which one are you?"

"What do you think?" she replied.

"A Tropher. And your power is to blind the foe," I joked.

"Very funny," she said sarcastically.

"By choosing their new owner, you mean they have a mind of their own?" I questioned.

"Exactly."

"So, the magic can talk to me?" She nodded.

I tried to reach out to my inner magic. I closed my eyes and spoke in my mind, "Hello, Magic. Are you there?" Nothing, I felt nothing. Just as I was about to ask Glint if I can talk to it, the truck suddenly stopped.

"Huh? Is there a fire?!" Leo jolted awake.

"Shhhhh! They'll hear us!" Glint warned.

We heard the front door opening and then closing. Voices could be heard from outside. "Hehe. Time to bring the loot in for some dolla dolla."

"Run when I give the signal," Glint ordered, getting up.

"What's the signal?" Leo asked, picking up Liz. Way earlier than expected, the door opened. Early morning sunlight streamed in. Glint's glittering wears saved us. Wow! What a weird thing to say!

Bobby and Mark were blinded by the shimmer of Glint, "What's that light?!"

"Run!" yelled Glint.

I took off before thinking. Mark or Bobby, I couldn't make out which, groaned as I bumped into him. I came to my senses and saw Glint and Leo in front of me.

"Faster!" yelled Glint.

I moved my legs faster. We were on the side of the highway. Because it was so early, there were no cars. We ran down a turn. There was a sign saying, 'Romdentia 30 miles ahead.' I smiled. At least we were close.

It was a short-lived happiness as I heard, "Get over there and catch them, Bobby! They have our loot."

I ran as fast as my little thin sticks called 'legs' could move. Glint and Leo jumped out of the highway into a dense forest. Hesitantly, I followed.

Chapter 11

DIN

Rolling in the mud, I tried to keep my head protected. I've seen this tutorial on how to protect yourself if you ever find yourself rolling at high speeds. Don't know why.

I got up and patted myself down to see if anything was broken. I looked around but there was no one there.

The trees were clumped up, barely letting any sunlight through. It was so beautiful that I wished I could stay and admire the view, but I could not waste any time. I had to find Glint and Leo.

I called out their names. But there was no response. I ventured in further; I came across something like a cave. I was creeped out more than ever. But they might have gone in there. As I walked in, my feet crunched the dry leaves on the ground.

"Ahhhhh," I heard a short shrill scream. That kind of sounded like Leo. I had no choice.

I ran into the cave, "Leo? Leoooo?" I yelled.

"Over here!" that was Glint! I came to a stop at a fork turn. Which way do I go? My thoughts pondered my head. While I was here, they might be in all kinds of trouble. Maybe there was a monster roasting them for dinner. Or maybe they were holding them for ransom, though I don't know what they would do with human money. I really don't think they can go to Walmart and buy some fruits.

I decided that taking the right is always right. I went into the right path hoping it would be that one. The cave was made of stone. There were no cracks whatsoever. It looked too…planned? I don't think an actual cave would be like this. Caves usually have insects and other lots of tiny critters, this one had not one in sight. Not that I could see much anyway. There was little to no light. I was feeling helpless. What could a kid do in this situation? Maybe, I should just go back and call the police.

I imagined Glint with me right now. She would scold me for being too scared. She was right. I need to do this. Come on, Sam! Get your head in the game!

"Sam!" Glint called as if telepathically she knew I was thinking about her.

I tried to follow the voice as best I could. I ran at full speed in the dark and hit a dead end, literally! After a few minutes, I seemed to be in the right place. It was a big hallway. It led straight to a cavern. I thought that's where Glint and Leo were trapped. I walked slowly. I came to the cavern. It had a ridiculously high ceiling curving to meet the walls. Big spikes were threatening to fall with every move I took.

"Sam!" I heard once again. I was now confident that I was in the correct place. I cautiously took a step forward. Nothing happened. I slowly trudged into the cavern. Something was curled up in the center—something very large and swirly. It looked like it had shiny skin. I went closer.

Normally, I would have figured it out. But then, it was dark. I could almost touch it now. I reached out. I know that this is the part where everyone shouts "Don't do it!" and the main character does it anyway and gets in a sticky situation after. Well, I did exactly that. My fingers contacted the thing. A bit too late, I realized that it looked like a snake! I couldn't pull away in time and I touched it.

I expected that it would be wet and fleshy. But instead, it was completely dry. It crumpled to dust from the point I touched. It was shed skin of a snake! Slowly, I backed away. Hopefully, the thing that had this as its former skin was not still here. I turned around. But guess what! The gods said that this boy has had rotten luck all the time, let's not change that!

"Ssssss."

SAM LOOKS AT DIN THE SNAKE

With terror on my face, I turned around again. A giant snake was towering over me. It was at least three stories tall. It had one eye as big as me. But then again, that was not saying much. The eye was very grey. As if a storm was trapped in the eyeball. I froze. I was too scared to breathe.

The snake simply stood there without moving. Maybe, it was friendly. It did not do anything to hurt me yet. I took a slow step back and the moment my toes came in contact with that floor, the snake lunged at me. It was lightning fast. I was very surprised when I dropped on the floor. The snake barely clipped the top of my hair. I could not get up. My legs were frozen. I guess that's why I fell. The sight of the snake moving made my legs go, "Yeah okay, that's it. I can't take no more."

The snake, again, stood where it got up from the spot it crashed on the ground. Again, I tried to move. But, that was a huge mistake. It moved. I blinked due to being scared, obviously. And the next thing I knew was the two long teeth up close.

Chapter 12

AM I DEAD?

Suddenly, I was cased in the dark. I got up on my feet. It was pitch black. I couldn't see my hand in front of me. What had happened? I thought. Maybe, I died. I had read stories. I am supposed to go in the light at the end of the tunnel to enter a new life. But there was no light and was I even in a tunnel?

Well, I was a failure. I had failed to save my parents. I had failed to save Glint and Leo. Strike that, I had failed to save myself. I sat down. It was slimy, the floor. Tears rolled down my cheeks. How had I believed that I could save my parents? I was just a child. Maybe, I should have called the police. As I sat there in misery, I heard a voice.

"Sam?" I looked around there was no one. I could not see one foot in front of me, of course. I got up and went further. I saw the shine. Finally, the light had come. I walked to the light. I could finally pass from this life and start a new one. The light was very close now. And bright. Very bright.

"Sam," the light called to me. I reached out with my hands. A hand reached out and grabbed mine. Somebody screamed. Okay, it was me. My eyes settled and I saw Glint. Yeah, Glint.

"Glint? What are you doing here?"

"Just lost my way to the restroom," she said, "what do ya think?"

"Sam?" I looked over to the other voice. It was Leo.

"Okay, so what are you doing here?" I asked. "Did you die too?"

"What?" Glint asked. "We are not dead. We are in this dang snake."

For a few seconds, I thought that Glint had gone crazy. Uh, crazier than before. And that was saying a lot.

"This is the den of Din." The realization hit me. That's why Din, the snake, only attacked me when I moved, it could hear my feet. Glint had told me that it relied on smell and sound. It smelled me come in. That is kind of ironic since snakes can't smell or hear. Not properly at least. Did you know snakes can smell with their tongue and hear only low frequencies? They hear what we hear but very muffled, like someone has their faces stuffed in between a sofa and trying to speak. I read this in a book once.

Anyways, I stood there in silence for a while.

"Are you telling me that," I took a deep breath, "the snake…the SNAKE ate me and now, I'm snake food?!" I was done now; rage was filling inside me. My eyes were twitching. Go ahead and say that I have cyclothymia (mood swings). One second, I'm crying and depressed and the next I'm raging on about how a snake ate me.

"I can't believe this!" I stomped. "Are you telling me that I went all the way, reached this far and failed? I almost crashed. Wait a minute, I did. Not to mention the way I became a stowaway on a hunter's truck. This is the worst!" I sat back down, breathing heavily. Leo and Glint had taken several steps back and were staring.

"Umm, Sam?"

"What?" I said. I saw what they were looking at. It was me. "What? Is there something on my face?" I touched my face, feeling it. There was nothing weird. I looked down. My body was gray. No, glowing gray. My eyes widened. I scanned my hands and the rest of my body. Everything was glowing gray. Or more like silver.

"What is happening?" Leo asked. We just stood there for a while.

Glint was the first one to snap out of it, "First, we have to get out of here." She had a worried look on her face. She removed a hidden knife from her shoe and started to look around.

"You had that the whole time?" Leo asked, looking frustrated. "You mean we could have gotten out a long time ago!"

"We can't stab it," Glint said as if that were supposed to explain everything.

I said what Leo and I were thinking, "I don't understand."

She sighed. "This is Din we are talking about. He is very strong, from the inside, too. Many people have tried to get out from the inside but don't realize that weapons are practically useless if you are dealing with Din."

"So, what are you doing with that knife?"

"Tickling it," she said.

Again, Leo and I were confused.

"I don't think we should question it as long as it works," Leo muttered as I was about to ask.

"Don't try to fix what ain't broken," I agreed.

Glint stretched her hand back and launched it as hard as possible. A hit like that was sure to cut through the flesh but to my surprise, it barely scratched the skin. The snake suddenly moved and all of us fell down.

"Is it working?" I asked.

"Yes. Now get to work." Glint pulled out a knife from her sleeve. And then she removed one out of her shoe. Leo and I were staring at her.

"How many knives do you have?"

"Well, one in my pocket. One in my jacket. And a smaller one up my sleeve. A big one up my other sleeve. And-"

"Okay, that's enough. Now let's start stabbing!" Leo whooped, "I always wanted to stab something!"

"Did you know that Leo had a dark side?" I muttered to no one.

I took a knife from Glint and got in position; Leo did the same.

"On three," Leo said, "One, two, three!"

We swung our hands as hard as we could. Suddenly, I felt like I was on a roller coaster. I was tumbling around. I tucked my head in the protection of my hands and knees.

"Keep trying to stab. But be careful, you might hit someone," said Glint. Leo and I tried to but only Glint succeeded without hitting any of us. After a while, just before my last meal was about to come up, we were dumped out and I fell down on my butt, but I was too dizzy to get up.

The first thing I noticed was that I was glowing brighter than ever, not that I usually glowed. It was almost white now.

SAM, GLINT AND LEO MOVING INTO THE REALM OF SHADOWS

The second thing I noticed was that we were not in the same place where Din swallowed us. Emphasis on not. We were on a seemingly floating island. Floating as in there was a big black void, almost like space but without the stars. Just endless black. There were some more floating islands in the distance, though.

And the third thing I noticed was the island we were in; there were torches all over but with blue fire instead of the usual fiery red.

"There," a slithery voice behind us said. "Now give me my reward and I ssshall leave. You know these ones were tricky to catch, I almost dumped them out in between because they kept tickling me. Fast now, I don't like this dark land."

I tried to stand up but found out that my arms were tied up; so were Glint's and Leo's. I couldn't stretch my neck to look behind.

"You will get your reward soon enough. Don't worry," a second male voice said.

"Good work," this time it was a female voice.

"Don't addressss me as a common servant. I only do work for me and this does not mean we are friendsss. Don't you dare think like that!"

"Gee! Okay, okay. I won't."

"Hey! Where am I? Let me out!" Leo yelled. He squirmed in his ropes.

Glint was suspiciously quiet. Which was quite unlike her.

"What is this place? Let me go!" Leo sounded scared.

I caught a glance at Glint. It looked like she was trying really hard to concentrate, and Leo was not helping.

I elbowed Leo. "Shut up!" He looked at me and was taken aback.

"Woah! Why are you glowing?"

I shushed him.

I really hoped Glint could work her magic and get us out of here. Till then, I tried to think of a backup plan. I had a knife—the one Glint had given; I could try to cut the ropes. I looked at Leo and saw that he was way ahead of me. He already had his knife out and was struggling to cut the ropes.

"What about these guys, now," said the man.

"The royalties had said to bring the prisoners to them."

"That's weird. The last Safion we caught was taken straight to Sateran."

I looked at Glint and tried very hard to scream. Sadly, a squeak escaped my mouth.

Glint was radiating orange and yellow. It felt like she was giving off the warmth and comfort of the sun. I strangely felt very relaxed, like I had no care in the world. All I wanted to do was just lie down and gaze up with no thoughts running in my mind. A small part of my mind told me, "You are here on a mission! This is no time for sleeping!"

Oh yeah, I was here with a purpose.

"Stop dreaming, dude!"

"Whoa, who was that?"

"You have to resist. If you don't you are done for!"

It felt like it was in my head. No matter where I turned, it was with the same volume.

Who are you? I tried to speak back to it. I was gaining a bit more presence. Still dazed, though.

"It is no time for questions. You have to trust me! Just try to block out the magic. I will help you."

The voice was comforting. It made me trust it. I thought about why I was here—to save my parents. I thought about Leo and Glint, trying to gain as much clarity as I could.

It felt like hours before the pressure was released from my mind and the thoughts came rushing back to me. I was still tied up. But I looked around and saw Glint breathing heavily. Leo was lying down. I looked back and saw the man and woman who had been talking, sleeping soundly. I saw Glint reach and pull a knife from God knows where. She cut the ropes and got up shakily.

I was at a loss for words, I realized that the relaxed feelings were her magic. If I had not listened to that voice and resisted, I would have never found myself again.

I wondered where the slithery voice, probably the snake that ate us, went.

"W-what happened?" Leo asked, looking dazed.

Glint was quiet as she cut Leo's ropes. Leo then realized, "Wow," he said softly.

It looked like he had more questions but wisely kept his mouth shut; the magic had clearly taken a toll on Glint.

She cut me free.

"What now?"

"Now, that those two have failed, I will have to take you to the king and queen so that I get my reward!" The slithery voice that belonged to the snake was the last thing I heard before being gobbled up again.

Chapter 13

THE KING AND QUEEN

I really hate being swallowed by snakes, especially the large ones. It just isn't my thing.

So, there I was, tumbling around in a familiar inside. I really didn't know why this time Din kept the ride bumpy, maybe to stop us from tickling him again.

"Noo! I hate this!" Leo complained.

I realized that if you concentrate on one thing and close your eyes, it helps with the feeling of motion sickness.

After tumbling around for a while, it stopped.

I found Glint and Leo.

"Should we stab it again?" Leo asked.

"No," Glint said. "The snake is taking us to the king and queen. That must be where Sam's parents must be. But I warn you, Sam. They must be holding your parents hostage to negotiate the trade of your powers. They know you won't be able to say no. They have been known to be iniquitous like that."

I nodded, pretending to know what that word meant. Glint wasn't wrong though; I wouldn't be able to say no when they offer my parents like that.

"So, then what?"

She didn't have time to answer that as we were dumped out. Again. Did I mention I hate getting swallowed by snakes?

We were again on a similar island. Except it was much larger than the one before. There were way more blue torches. There were huge buildings. None of them were higher than two stories. But they were covering way more span on the ground. It was bright, thanks to the flames.

The buildings were surprisingly full and bustling. But there was something weird. I looked closer. Squinting my eyes, I saw that the people were different. They had blue fire-like eyes. And their bodies were like dancing shadows. Nobody could have noticed it if they hadn't been looking closely. I looked over at Glint to ask but stopped in my tracks. She was like that, too. Except her eyes were green. I looked at Leo and he was looking at me, with a similar look on his face.

"What?" I asked, "What is it?"

I understood. I looked down and to my horror, I was a shadow, only for a moment though. It was like I was flickering into a human and then back again. Only Leo looked normal.

I guessed that I was glowing probably because of the Safion thing. I looked around taking in the ironic beauty. I could hear Leo shaking behind me.

"It's ok," I assured.

"Are you kidding me?" Leo said. "This is probably the most exciting thing that is ever going to happen to me." Well, I guess that was Leo.

Glint looked at me and said, "Follow the plan."

I wanted to say, "What plan?"

But Leo beat me to it. "We don't even have a plan!"

"Just cooperate and get me some time."

"Move it. I want my reward," said the snake. Din shoved us with its giant head.

"If you try anything, I will make sure that will be the last thing you do."

We walked past lots of shadows. They looked at us and seemed quite hostile. But every time a shadow came near us Din would get in their face and show off his huge teeth. Needless to say, no one bothered us after that.

They seemed extremely amazed when they saw me and I was not enjoying the attention.

Glint looked determined. Leo looked like he had seen the most amazing thing in the world. I looked like I had just seen my brother on the toilet.

After what felt like an hour of walking and getting amazed, we were standing at the gates of a huge castle. And by huge, I mean enormous.

I swear I could hear Leo's jaw drop to the floor.

Din tried to walk us in but the guards stopped us.

"What business might you have with a human." He said 'human' as if it were a forbidden word.

"And with a Zedexian."

"Oh, trust me," said Din. "The royals will want to see this." He shoved me in front of the guard. "Look closer."

The guard gasped. He opened the gate at once.

"Wait, take this." He gave us cards to hang over our necks. They said, "Hello! I am a visitor."

Glint wore it reluctantly.

I guess this was not much different from back on Earth. I bet children also came here for school trips. Huh, when I look at it like that, I guess they are not much different from us. After all, we humans *are* supposed to be copies of them. So, I could say that *we* are like them.

The doors of the castle opened by themselves; of course, they were too big and heavy for anyone to move. We entered a huge hallway. It wasn't even that bad. There were portraits all over as we walked down the hall. I suddenly stopped at one of the giant pictures. I could feel that I recognized the pitch-black shape of a man and woman, they were sitting on a gold throne. If I wasn't focusing on the photo I could see their faces and they looked very familiar. But I couldn't put my finger on it.

We reached the end of a hallway which had a very grand-looking door. The doors boomed and opened. Two people standing on the end of a carpet were shadows. Then, I realized who they were.

Chapter 14

MY 'PARENTS'

*N*ot in my wildest dreams I would have imagined this. My knees buckled and I was a second from fainting. They were my parents.

My mind did not know what to do, I didn't know if I should be angry, sad or both. But my worries seemed to fade when she spoke to me.

"I'm sorry," said my mother. She approached me and touched my face. It was too difficult to not sympathize with the eyes that were filled with sorrow and despair. She was my mother. She loved me more than anything in the world. The feeling was quite mutual.

I looked straight into those extremely dark eyes. In normal circumstances, I would not have been so trusting, but I don't know, it was like Glint's magic except it was more forcing. Of course, I didn't realize this at the time.

"I could go back, you know," she said. "We could go back." She looked at Dad. He looked longingly at me. "All you have to do is give up your magic."

My 'Parents'

Glint was right, of course, she was. But she said that she had a plan. But then again, I really did want my parents back. I still couldn't accept the fact that they were shadows. How could they keep it from me? If they wanted my magic, they could have asked without leaving. I would have gladly given it to them. But now I had my doubts after I knew what was at stake. Why had they sent Sateran after me? I had thousands of questions. This just didn't add up. But of course, my brain was melted by seeing my parents.

My dad walked to me and mom moved aside, still looking at me.

"You won't even use it. It will be a win-win. You will be able to lead a normal life with the shadows. And shadows will reclaim Earth. Weren't you always complaining that you can't fit in?"

I have always been known to be pushy. I could not accept anything without knowing for sure. It was the reason I quite liked science; nothing was definite till it was proven.

"Why did you not tell me that you were shadows? And that I was a Safion?"

"Well, we were not sure that you would take the news well. So, we had you see it for yourself."

"Did you send Glint to me? Was this all staged? Din, too, was given orders?"

Dad eyed Din to stay quiet—which I realized only later

I was being less and less on board with the idea of giving up my powers.

"Why did you send Sateran after me? Why did he want to kill me? He promised to train me with my powers. But you want me to give up my powers. Why?"

"Sam, listen-" my mom was saying but I cut her off.

"No! You listen. If you are both shadows, then how am I a Safion—half human?"

"Sam-" she tried again but I was on a roll now.

"Wrong! Mom never-never calls me Sam! Only 'honey'! And shadows can't pass into the universe. You really are not my parents, are you? I bet my parents are somewhere tied up!"

By the end, I was panting heavily. But I felt like I could never stop. I could feel my blood rushing through my veins. I was aware of Leo's breathing. I felt like I was alive for the first time.

I could see a bit of fear in their eyes, but they hid it fast. I noticed that I was glowing cyan, instead of silver.

"Very well," said Dad—no, king. "If you want to do this the hard way…"

My 'Parents'

SHADOW KING AND QUEEN FIGHTING SAM AND GLINT

The king and queen suddenly changed and they reappeared, with crowns and they wore a long flowing cape which looked like it was made from blue fire.

Before they could do anything, I yelled, "Glint!"

And so, the chaos broke out.

Chapter 15

I FINALLY USE MY MAGIC SOMEHOW

Glint touched the floor and at the point where she touched, a giant crack swelled towards the king. The king held out his hand and a blue ball of energy formed. But before it could leave his hands, the crack in the floor, which was like a snake beneath them, reached the king.

A giant spike made of wood erupted from his feet and threw him hard on the very high ceiling.

"Oof!" the King gasped. "I was not ready for that!"

Then, Glint touched the wall and vines grew around the king and trapped him. But what shocked me was that he just turned into his shadow form and fazed through it. It seemed very easy for him.

"Ha! You thought I was that easy?" he continued to throw light balls at Glint.

Glint focused and pressed her hand on the ground. The king saw this as a distraction and ran towards her. I quickly went in for a shoulder push to slam him into the wall. But he was ready for it. I put my full force into it. But he just turned into a shadow. And I just crumbled on the wall.

He had almost reached Glint. Slowly, something wiggled out of the ground, glowing brightly. The king skidded to a stop.

"A sun worm! Foolish girl, you have doomed us all!" his shadow started to hiss and burn. He tried to get away but tripped. The sun worm approached the king. "Plan: Five.O.Y.E!" he yelled out and disappeared. The Sun worm went back into the ground and Glint panted.

Glint and I did not know what those words meant but they seemed to have a load of meaning to the Queen who was hidden behind the thrones to avoid the sun worm's shine.

"You can't be serious!" she said. She looked at me and made a big blue ball very fast.

"You will pay," she threw the ball at me. I don't know what happened but with instinct, I stomped my foot and a tree grew in front of me extremely fast.

The tree was bursting with cyan light. The moment the blue ball hit it, we were all shrouded in light. When the light faded, we saw the queen in crumbles.

"This is not the last of us you will see," she said and disappeared into the ground.

I was confused. How had I destroyed the queen when I only blocked the attack? My confusion was cleared up when Leo appeared from a blue portal on top of Din. He had a selfie stick in his hand and wore sunglasses. The portal looked a lot like the portal Doctor Strange opened in the movies.

Leo must have known what I was thinking because he said,

"Where else do you think they got the idea from?"

"Where were you?" I asked. "And why do you have a selfie stick?"

He must be reading my mind. I was going to ask next about what he was doing. He was not there the entire time we fought.

"I convinced Din to fight for us. He hates it when they don't pay him. So, when you all couldn't see in the light, I smacked the queen in the head. Honestly, I was kind of bored of her talking."

"This is a temporary alliance only," said Din, "don't expect us to be friends. Now, I must go, I must catch up on some of Snakes and Ladders."

"Thank you for your help, and I understand."

I don't know if it was my imagination or not, but I think I saw the faintest smile on Din's face.

The blue portal opened but Din didn't go through the portal.

"Your parents will be found in there," he said.

"How do you know?" I asked.

"Rule one of businesssss with suspicious people is to have a weapon if they refuse to keep up with their bargain. And the Trophers can be shady," Din winked (I think he winked, since you know, he had only one eye) and said, "Pun intended." With that, he opened a different portal and went through it.

"I don't think we should trust him," said Glint.

"Yeah," I agreed, "I think he was kind of dodgy. What if it is a trap? We don't even know what that plan five something was!"

Leo was looking offended, "No way! He helped us with the Queen."

In the halls, we heard rapid footsteps. "Whatever we do, we have to do it fast," I spoke. "Looks like the guards are coming."

"We should stay here," said Glint. "We might get trapped in there forever." She looked at Leo with a look that said, "So much for your trust in Din."

A crowd of shadows flooded through the doors. "We can do it," I said.

More shadows came through the doors. I looked at Leo and Glint. We came to a silent agreement.

"Yeah, no way." We all jumped through the portal.

Chapter 16

THE PUZZLE ROOM

*W*e tumbled through the portal and the first thing I saw was that we were in a room—not very big, but empty. It was dark though.

"Oof," fell Leo.

"Leo, move I'm here," Glint said.

"Okay."

"No, not there, that's my foot."

"Sorry."

"My other foot! Leo!"

"My bad."

Glint grunted and next, I heard Leo fall to the floor. It appeared as though Glint had enough and shoved Leo off her.

"Where are we?" asked Leo. "And how are we going back?"

Honestly, I had no idea. But I wasn't going to say that. He might panic.

"You have no idea," he said, "do you?"

Again, I had the impression that he could read my mind.

"That's not true," I said defensively, "Din said that this would lead to my parents. So, it must be kind of a puzzle room. we must find a way out of here." I looked at Leo with an accomplished look on my face.

"And how do we get out of here?"

"Umm, I'll think of that later."

"Oh, really? We-"

A scrapping noise erupted. We looked and saw a doorway forming out of stone which the room was made from. Glint was standing right beside it.

We stared.

"What are you looking at?" she said. "Now let's go! It's not like your parents are growing any younger!" she walked in.

Leo just shrugged and went after her. And I went after him.

Inside, I saw my parents sitting on the floor. I was overjoyed to see them.

"Mom? Dad?" I said.

"They're asleep," Leo said. "We will have to carry them. This leads me to my question, how the heck will we get out of here!"

Again, I had no idea. But Glint looked like she did.

"I can open a portal like Din did but I can't do it alone." She looked at me.

"No way! I don't have the faintest idea how to. That back there was instinct. Even if I did try, we might end up in, I don't know, Australia?"

There never was a plan I heard in which so many things could go wrong.

"Or...," Leo said, "we could just use this stone I got from Din." He pulled out something you could barely call a stone. It was closer to a pebble. It was glowing, very dimly though.

Glint gasped. "You had that the whole time? You should have said something. It's all most out of energy. I am going to strangle you!"

She reached for Leo. He came hid behind me.

"She is scary!" he told me.

Glint continued to make furious grabs at Leo.

"Guys, stop. What matters now is that we can get out of here. Even if we got worried because someone conveniently forgot to tell us that he—I mean, they—had the stone."

"Okay, so how does this work?" Leo asked. Glint still looked like she wanted to lay hands on Leo.

"Well, touch the stone and think about the place you want to go. Make sure to think of the same place, or it could go wrong. Your parents don't count. Since they are sleeping, they aren't thinking of anything."

I nodded. Getting my parents to touch the stone was work. I never knew that my dad's hand was so heavy.

"When I say 'now.' Okay?"

"Yeah," I said.

"One… two … now!"

I was caught off guard I barely had time to think about my house before I got a spinning feeling. All I could see was pitch black. I couldn't even see Leo and Glint.

Chapter 17

LEO'S CARS

*A*fter what felt like forever, I was standing again. But not at my house; it was Leo's porch.

"What?" I said. "I thought about my house. Why are we here?"

"I thought about my house," said Leo.

"Yeah, but Glint and I thought about my house," I looked at Glint.

"What? There were snacks here!"

I just rolled my eyes.

"So, how are we going to get my parents home before they wake up?"

"You could use one of my parent's cars," said Leo. "And have you noticed that this is around the same time we entered the shadow realm?"

Now that I thought about it, it was.

"Obviously," said Glint, "time works differently there."

"Anyways, where is the car, Leo?"

After we had set my parents on Leo's fancy sofa, Leo said, "Follow me."

We went to what looked like the garage. He walked in front of the door and it opened automatically.

"*Welcome, Leo.*"

Glint looked alarmed. "Who's there?" she took a ninja pose.

I laughed. "Relax, it's just the robot assistance."

Not for the first time I was surprised at how rich Leo was. Inside, there were five cars. All of them were deep purple. All of them looked very posh. There was one Porsche, two Rolls-Royce and three very 90s-looking cars. I'm sure you'll understand my reaction as a sucker for cars.

"Woah," my jaw dropped. "Th-these c-cars are s-s-so beautiful."

I was so shocked my mouth was betraying me. Leo just laughed and patted my back.

He walked to the three ancient-looking cars.

"We can't take these three, they are antiques. Priceless."

A high-pitched squeak escaped my mouth.

"Let's take that one," Glint pointed at the Porsche.

"Good choice," Leo took the keys from a rack.

EPILOGUE

The car ride home was uneventful. I managed to convince Leo to ride. I think I've had enough of Glint's driving to last me a lifetime. I kept thinking though, it all seemed too easy. The castle was practically unguarded. And the queen and king were defeated so easily. The room that Din led us through was also very easy to crack, either that or Glint was very smart. I think both.

And I still hadn't forgotten about the plan that the King said. Should I have been worried? I don't know.

We reached home and set my parents on the bed, I asked Glint, "Where are you going to go? I don't think you can go back to the shadow realm, can you?" She shook her head.

"You can always stay at my house," Leo offered. "I'm sure my folks won't mind."

"Thanks, but I have it all managed. And Sam, ask me if I ever need to save anyone again," she smiled. Glint had really grown a lot through our adventure. She is no longer the bossy irritable person.

"I should go now," Leo said. "It's getting dark."

I waved.

Epilogue

"I should go too," Glint said. She saw the sad look on my face. "Don't worry, we are not done saving humanity. And you can't get rid of me that easily."

She opened a portal and stepped through it.

"Hey, Leo!" I ran up to him. "I realized that nobody explained anything to you. About Glint and me and the shadows. Why did you not ask?"

He chuckled. "Well, I picked up everything along the way. I'm good at that kind of stuff." He got in the car and waved at me. "See you at school tomorrow."

Epilogue

I waved back.

Even if the adventure was easy, I didn't mind. I was lucky to have friends like Glint and Leo.

Is this the last adventure with them? I think not.

The End.

www.ingramcontent.com/pod-product-compliance
Lightning Source LLC
LaVergne TN
LVHW041543070526
838199LV00046B/1818